your mother looks good . . .

your mother looks good . . .

tim, phyllis & bob
MikWright, Ltd.

**Andrews McMeel
Publishing**

Kansas City

your mother looks good . . .

www.mikwright.com

05 RDS 10 9 8 7 6 5 4

ISBN-13: 978-0-7407-1411-5
ISBN-10: 0-7407-1411-2

Library of Congress Catalog Card Number: 00-108475

we dedicate *your mother looks good* . . .
to the maternal people of the world,
be they mothers, grandmothers, or sissy uncles,
who lay foundations for the next generation.
thank you!

acknowledgments

your mother looks good . . . is a continuation of tim and phyllis's best work from their wildly successful greeting card line featuring family photos combined with forked-tongued wit. when not dumpster diving for shipping boxes, tim and phyllis, along with fellow goof-off bob, work on telling it like it is.

we acknowledge the following because we have been threatened:

to our many gluers (adhesive specialists): stop sniffing and glue!

to lisa: you may be tall and you may be beautiful and, yes, you may have laid much groundwork for our success, but . . .

f.t.l.o.g., you feed your cats on the kitchen counter and that is just wrong!

to "just say julie": you started a craze by supplying us with chicken parts, enriched buns, and gay-mode panty hose bags from your insect-ridden attic.

p.s. white after labor day is a sin!

your mother looks good . . .

your mother looks good, but
your father looks better.

i couldn't give a shit if i tried.

that nutty heather, our diamond in the rough.

the story goes that her mother, judy, a '60s throwback, would just whip out the potty chair whenever and wherever necessary. today heather is a dancer and choreographer, as well as a high-profile MikWright gluer.

heather's life is a sitcom waiting to be written.

your mother sure knows how to work a crowd.

this is the same car that was recently seen
screaming away from sunrise manor nursing home.
irma nelson was later apprehended
trying to pawn six patchwork quilts
and a vibrating lounger.

eldora couldn't resist a chance
to look at leona's half-exposed breast.

mildred, eunice, and elaine met last saturday in downtown lancaster for lunch at the chat and chew café. all hell broke loose when elaine started choking on an asparagus tip. mildred got her emergency procedures screwed up and began mouth to mouth. well, you can imagine the rumors that started.

kent is now eleven and still wets the bed.
danny turns eight in january and is failing
remedial math class. timmy, our six-year-old,
only answers to "jessica."

haven't we all had enough of our friends'
holiday brag letters?

as it turns out, kent is an educator and
farmer, danny is a heating/cooling installer,
and timmy is writing so-called humor (when not
ordering crap from late-night infomercials).

from the looks of it, mom had us dressed for
handing out bibles while riding from lutheran
home to lutheran home in southwest minnesota.

. . . and then that bitch had the nerve to show up with jello instead of her assigned chicken casserole. now, i'm not one to gossip, but can you believe how fat she has gotten; bitch, please!

you're damn right i'm thirsty! now which one
of those things makes cappuccino?

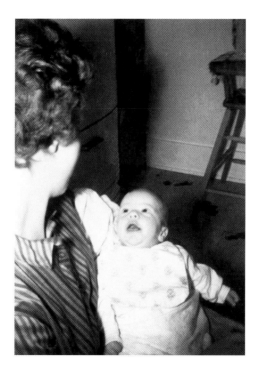

so help me god lorraine, if elected, my first
duty will be to reinstate nude bowling.

can't you just imagine sitting next to
"mouth" on a greyhound bound for austin?

for the life of me, i don't know how i got
that yeast infection. i was in and out of the
bakery in less than a minute.

what a good sport, that leona.

as one of twelve kids of a swedish immigrant, mom tells the story about getting a squeaky little doll for christmas the same year that her brother howard got a pocket knife. so, as you may have guessed, howard cut open her only present to see what made the noise.

howard later got his payback when he ran the tractor into the house as he tried to scare leona, who was looking out the kitchen window.

you didn't want to be around madge when
it was that time of the month. period.
end of discussion.

don't look so sad, eunice. it makes me equally
upset to have someone call me "sir."

the competition at daytona was tight.
lucky for dorinda, judy misplaced
her thigh crème.

news flash charlotte . . .

your "you-know-what" does stink!

come on in!
i'm sorry, but robert's got diarrhea
and the kids both have lice, so . . . it's
just going to be us. i hope you're hungry.

melissa is our little bob's mommy. voted prettiest mother at parents' day in third grade, melissa often single-handedly reared four kids while her military husband brought home the bacon. not only could this '60s mother keep a house and dazzle the family with a standing rib roast, but her swing on the golf course would put to shame most of the plaid-pants men in the clubhouse.

there still seems to be family issues over the forced consumption of spam with at least three of the four siblings.

don't look now, jeanette, but is that her ass
or did they raise the titanic?

you know i'm not wearing any underwear.

excuse me ma'am, we cannot leave the gate
until you're seated . . . and from the looks
of that ass, this flight is canceled!

after a collective fifty years in the airline industry, tim, phyllis, and bob have heard and seen it all. believe us, we bit our tongue more times than we'd like to remember. a few stories, some unsubstantiated, follow:

passenger talking into overhead speaker
to order a soda.

human remains shipment (corpse) used
as a picnic table.

cargo shipment of five hundred baby chicks
loose on the runway.

man sitting in the first-class toilet cracked the door and asked the flight attendant to retrieve his book.

male flight attendant caught trying on a woman's bobcat fur coat.

woman breast-feeding a kitten (in economy class, no doubt).

although a miracle, mary regretted
not having an epidural.

she had a face only a mother could love.
sound familiar?

i don't know about the rest of the joneses, but i do know about miss jones and keeping up with her is a full-time job. if you've got something to say . . . so does she, but that's what we love about miss jones.

three words . . . piece of work!

i ran into so many pricks that day
i thought i was at my family reunion.

i ain't got no list, santa.
but, could you bring mama a complete set of
teeth, a veg-o-matic, and a fifth of vodka?

get with it lenny!

when i said i needed a napkin i wasn't talking

about a moist towelette!

it was all about timothy and his
carousel cake—the perfect prelude to his
future stage name . . . "mary a go-go round."

aaah, the infamous carousel cake.
red drinking straws, a little cardboard hat,
some plastic ponies and i was happy.
mom got a lot of use out of that cake
decorating set. personally, i think i got
the cake five times as a kid (not that
i'm bitter).

about the authors . . . and bob.

tim mikkelsen is misunderstood. he's balding
and has been seen in places that would
make his parents change their underwear. tim
loves a vodka martini, straight-up, with
olives. phyllis, also known to partake of the
libations, aspires to rid the world of
electronic devices. if it were up to phyllis,
we would all be chipping notes in slate and
talking into cans connected with string.

both airline veterans, tim and phyllis laugh
at everything and take serious nothing.

. . . and bob. being control freaks, tim
and phyllis found it hard to let bob create
verse. but, much to everyone's surprise,
bob williams sobered up and whipped out
a classic about some woman's ass and the
titanic. look for more of . . . and bob!